JOHN LEWIS

THIS EDITION
Produced for DK by WonderLab Group LLC
Jennifer Emmett, Erica Green, Kate Hale, *Founders*

Editor Maya Myers; **Photography Editor** Nicole DiMella; **Managing Editor** Rachel Houghton; **Designers** Project Design Company; **Researchers** Michelle Harris, Debra Bodner; **Copy Editor** Lori Merritt; **Indexer** Connie Binder; **Proofreader** Susan K. Hom; **Sensitivity Reader** Ebonye Gussine Wilkins; **Series Reading Specialist** Dr. Jennifer Albro

First American Edition, 2025
Published in the United States by DK Publishing, a division of Penguin Random House LLC
1745 Broadway, 20th Floor, New York, NY 10019

Copyright © 2025 Dorling Kindersley Limited
24 25 26 27 10 9 8 7 6 5 4 3 2 1
001–345878–May/2025

Publisher's note: This book uses terms for Black Americans as appropriate to modern and historical contexts.
Historical terms are defined in the glossary.

All rights reserved.
Without limiting the rights under the copyright reserved above, no part of this publication may be reproduced, stored in or introduced into a retrieval system, or transmitted, in any form, or by any means (electronic, mechanical, photocopying, recording, or otherwise), without the prior written permission of the copyright owner.
Published in Great Britain by Dorling Kindersley Limited

A catalog record for this book is available from the Library of Congress.
HC ISBN: 978-0-5939-6637-2
PB ISBN: 978-0-5939-6636-5

DK books are available at special discounts when purchased in bulk for sales promotions, premiums, fund-raising, or educational use.
For details, contact:
DK Publishing Special Markets, 1745 Broadway, 20th Floor, New York, NY 10019
SpecialSales@dk.com

Printed and bound in China
Super Readers Lexile® levels 800L to 1010L
Lexile® is the registered trademark of MetaMetrics, Inc. Copyright © 2024 MetaMetrics, Inc. All rights reserved.

The publisher would like to thank the following for their kind permission to reproduce their images:
a=above; c=center; b=below; l=left; r=right; t=top; b/g=background
Alamy Stock Photo: Abaca Press / CNP / Ron Sachs 6bc, AP Photo / Floyd Edwin Jillson 51, AP Photo / Gregory Smith 44bl, AP Photo / Linda Schaeffer 50tl, AP Photo / Montgomery Advertiser, Mickey Welsh 30tl, AP Photo / Nashville Police Department 18tl, Associated Press 42b, 47br, dpa picture alliance / CNP / Chris Kleponis 23tr, Everett Collection Historical 14-15tl, 32b, 35, Everett Collection Inc 26-27t, Glasshouse Images / Circa Images 32tl, History of America 49c, IanDagnall Computing 36bl, Imago 60-61b, Jeffrey Isaac Greenberg 18+ 58bl, Keystone Pictures USA 20tl, NurPhoto SRL / Paul Hennessy 3, 15crb, Pictorial Press Ltd / Alamba Dept or Archives and History. 16b, RBM Vintage Images / National Archives of Fort Worth 46b, SBS Eclectic Images 22tl, SOPA Images Limited 60tl, UPI / Kevin Dietsch 56tl, Velvet Film / Album 40-41b, WENN Rights Ltd 58br, Jim West 18b, White House Photo 54tl; **Dreamstime.com:** Bestvc 25cra, Olga Bogatyrenko 52b; **Getty Images:** Archive Photos 49tl, Archive Photos / Daily Express / Hulton Archive 24-25t, Archive Photos / Stephen F. Somerstein 46br, Archive Photos / Villon Films / Robert Elfstrom 7, Bettmann 12, 17tr, 17br, 19t, 24cl, 25c, 27cr, 29bl, 30b, 31t, 38, 43br, 47tl, Corbis Historical / Leif Skoogfors 48tl, Corbis News / Mark Reinstein 55, Corbis Premium Historical / Steve Schapiro 34, 45cr, 48br, CQ-Roll Call, Inc. / Bill Clark 1, CQ-Roll Call, Inc. / Tom Williams 49tr, 52tl, 53t, 59tr, Express / Hulton Archive 22cla, fotog 37br, Heritage Images / Hulton Archive 45br, Hulton Archive / Kypros 33tl, Charles Moore 43t, Elijah Nouvelage 61tr, The Chronicle Collection / Don Cravens 11t, The Chronicle Collection / Don Uhrbrock 28, 29tr, The Washington Post / Jahi Chikwendiu 33 (11 mug shots), The Washington Post / Ted Richardson 14bl, Barry Williams 19cr, 58-59t, Mark Wilson 16tl; **Getty Images / iStock:** Inna Tarasenko 8cla, Becky Wright 6l; **IMAGN:** Jimmy Ellis 4-5, Jack Corn / The Tennessean - USA TODAY Network 22-23t, The Tennessean 21, USA TODAY NETWORK / Jimmy Ellis 17t; **John F. Kennedy Library Foundation:** Cecil Stoughton. White House Photographs. 36-37t; **LBJ Library:** White House Photo Office / Arnold Newman 40tl, White House Photo Office / Cecil Stoughton 42tl, White House Photo Office / Yoichi Okamoto 46tc; **Library of Congress, Washington, D.C.:** LC-DIG-fsa-8a03228 / Vachon, John, photographer 10b, LC-DIG-fsa-8b29589 / Lange, Dorothea, photographer 9tr, LC-DIG-ppmsca-08102 / Pettus, Peter, photographer 44-45t, LC-USF34-018335-D / Lange, Dorothea, photographer 8-9b, LC-USZ62-96308 26cla; **National Archives:** 36tl, 39tr; **Shutterstock.com:** Tiago Pestana 13; **U.S. government works:** Official White House Photo by Lawrence Jackson 57, Official White House Photo by Pete Souza 54br

Cover images: *Front:* **Alamy Stock Photo:** IanDagnall Computing; **Dreamstime.com:** Mesutdogan (Building);
Back: **Dreamstime.com:** Alejandro Duran cra; **Getty Images / iStock:** eyewave clb

All other images © Dorling Kindersley Limited
For more information see: www.dkimages.com

www.dk.com

This book was made with Forest Stewardship Council™ certified paper – one small step in DK's commitment to a sustainable future.
Learn more at
www.dk.com/uk/information/sustainability

Publisher's note: This book uses terms for Black Americans as appropriate to modern and historical contexts.
Historical terms are defined in the glossary.

Level 4

JOHN LEWIS

James Williams

CONTENTS

6	The Boy from Troy
14	Sit-Ins Begin
24	Freedom Riders
34	Youngest of the Big Six
40	Bloody Sunday and Beyond
48	Moving toward Government

52 The Conscience of Congress
62 Glossary
63 Index
64 Quiz

Police officers carry John Lewis away from a sit-in in Nashville

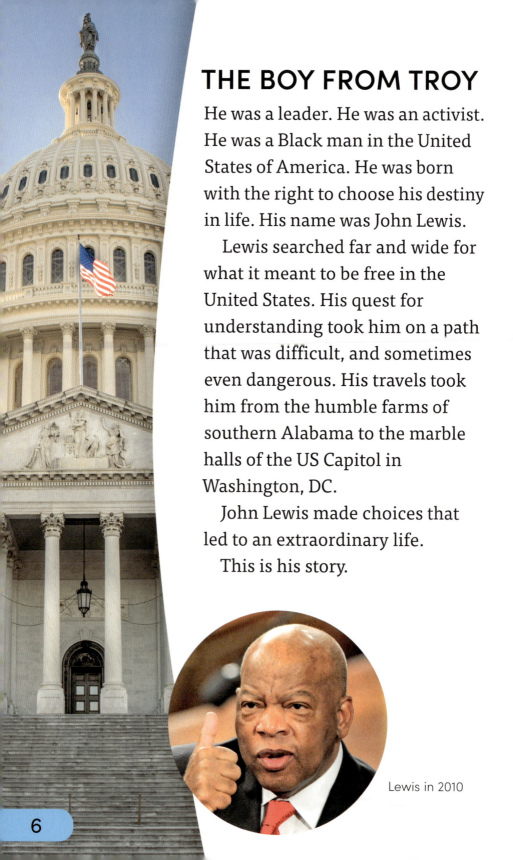

THE BOY FROM TROY

He was a leader. He was an activist. He was a Black man in the United States of America. He was born with the right to choose his destiny in life. His name was John Lewis.

Lewis searched far and wide for what it meant to be free in the United States. His quest for understanding took him on a path that was difficult, and sometimes even dangerous. His travels took him from the humble farms of southern Alabama to the marble halls of the US Capitol in Washington, DC.

John Lewis made choices that led to an extraordinary life.

This is his story.

Lewis in 2010

Lewis in 1964

John Lewis was born in 1940 near Troy, Alabama, an agricultural town. His parents were sharecroppers. He grew up in a close-knit community where earlier generations had been enslaved.

When John was four, a violent windstorm tore through his community. John and about 15 of his cousins and siblings took shelter in his aunt's house. The house shook.

A tenant farm in Alabama, 1938

They felt the storm lifting the corners of the house off the ground. John and his family held hands. They moved together from one corner to the next, holding the house down until the storm had passed.

John learned the importance of community and working with your family and friends. He carried this lesson with him for the rest of his life.

Later, John would come to believe that if all of America's people came together as a "beloved community," the nation could brave any storm.

Sharecropping
In return for allowing other people (sharecroppers) to farm on their land, landowners would get a share of the crops they grew. After the Civil War (1861–1865), many formerly enslaved people and their descendants became sharecroppers. Generally, the deals between landowners and sharecroppers were unfair to sharecroppers.

9

Jim Crow Laws
After the Civil War, enslaved people in America were set free. But some white people made laws to keep the races separated. These racist laws discriminated harshly against Black people and reinforced the power of white people.

John was born during one of many difficult periods for Black people in the US. This was the era of "Jim Crow" laws. They helped enforce segregation in the US from the late 19th century to the mid-20th century.

This troubled John from a young age. He knew that African Americans were citizens of the United States and believed that everyone should be treated the same. But everywhere John looked, his people were being treated unfairly.

Segregated drinking fountain in Halifax, North Carolina, 1938

Martin Luther King Jr.

When John was 15, 14-year-old Emmett Till was brutally murdered by two white men in Mississippi. The fear of such a thing happening to him felt like a prison to John.

Then, John heard civil rights leader Dr. Martin Luther King Jr. on the radio. King talked about resistance without violence. He said each person must speak up when they see something wrong happening—that they have an obligation to act. John liked these ideas.

> "One has not only a legal but a moral responsibility to obey just laws. Conversely, one has a moral responsibility to disobey unjust laws."
>
> —Martin Luther King Jr.

A segregated classroom in Virginia, 1947

Segregated Schools
In 1896, the US Supreme Court had ruled that races could be separate as long as they were equal. This made segregation legal. However, in 1954, the case *Brown v. Board of Education* said that separating children by race in schools was unconstitutional.

John attended segregated schools as a child. He applied to Troy State College (now Troy University), but he was denied admission because of his race. John wanted to sue the school for discrimination. He wrote to King, who invited John to meet him in Montgomery, the state capital. He warned John that a lawsuit could endanger his family. John decided not to pursue it. But he was determined to get an education.

He attended American Baptist Theological Seminary (now American Baptist College) in Nashville, Tennessee. He became a minister. Then, he attended Fisk University, an HBCU (historically Black college or university), where he earned a degree in religion and philosophy.

Celebrated Return

John would eventually be celebrated by the school that had denied him admission. In 1989, he received an honorary doctorate from Troy University. In 2018, the school and the city of Troy held a John Lewis Day in his honor.

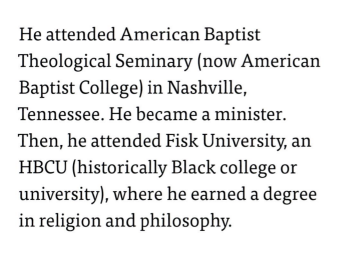

John Robert Lewis Hall, Troy University

A sit-in at a white-only lunch counter in Nashville, 1960

The Greensboro Four

In 1960, four students at North Carolina A&T State University staged a sit-in at a popular diner in downtown Greensboro, North Carolina. This act inspired similar protests nationwide.

SIT-INS BEGIN

In Nashville, Lewis was drawn to the struggle for civil rights. He wanted to stand up for racial equality. He met others who wanted to do the same. James Lawson, a master of nonviolent protest, became his mentor. Reverend Kelly Miller Smith and Bernard Lafayette also encouraged Lewis to take part in social activism. Soon, Lewis and his friends would begin making headlines.

(left to right) David Richmond, Franklin McCain, Ezell A. Blair Jr., and Joseph McNeil

14

On February 13, 1960, Lewis joined 124 college students from the Nashville Student Movement who were participating in sit-ins at popular diners in the city. They went to restaurants that refused to serve Black people. Defying this rule, they sat down and waited to be served. Their hope was to end segregation in the city.

Though the students were peaceful in their protests, many of them were assaulted by white people who wanted to stop the movement.

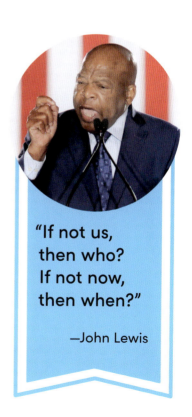

"If not us, then who? If not now, then when?"

—John Lewis

Even when they were met with hatred and violence, Lewis and his allies stayed calm and strong. They followed Lawson's nonviolent teachings. They were inspired by the examples set by King and Rosa Parks, who had led a successful bus boycott in Montgomery, Alabama, five years earlier. Faced with violence and insults, these leaders answered with nonviolence.

"You have to be taught the way of peace, the way of love, the way of nonviolence."

—John Lewis

Rosa Parks being fingerprinted during the bus boycott in Montgomery, 1956

O. D. Hunt, Dennis Foote, and Lewis (right) in jail after their arrest at a sit-in, March 25, 1960

Though the protesters in Nashville remained peaceful, dozens of students were arrested.

Nashville's jails were not meant to hold so many people at one time. Lewis and his allies knew this. They wanted to stay in jail. If it became too difficult to keep so many people in jail, they believed the city would have to make changes.

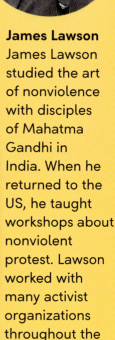

James Lawson
James Lawson studied the art of nonviolence with disciples of Mahatma Gandhi in India. When he returned to the US, he taught workshops about nonviolent protest. Lawson worked with many activist organizations throughout the civil rights movement.

Lewis's parents had always told him to not get into trouble. They didn't want him to put himself in danger. Yet Lewis took pride in being thrown in jail. He knew that people could not always avoid danger if they wanted to do the right thing. To make life better for his people, he would have to brave this trouble and much more.

Arrested
Lewis was arrested for peacefully protesting segregation 40 times between 1960 and 1966.

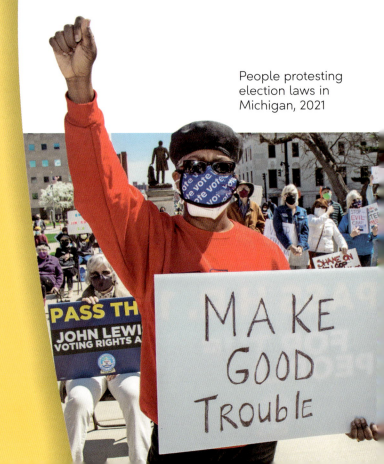

People protesting election laws in Michigan, 2021

Nashville mayor Ben West addressing protesting students, April 1960

Some trouble was worth getting into, Lewis felt. Later in his life, he would come to call this "good trouble."

While Lewis and his allies were fighting to end segregation, many white residents of Nashville wanted to keep the city segregated. They demanded that the mayor, Ben West, do something. West created a committee of Black and white leaders. Together, they agreed on a partial desegregation. They suggested that lunch counters be divided into Black and white sections.

The students were not willing to accept this offer. Their protests continued.

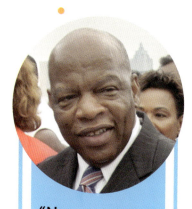

"Never, ever be afraid to make some noise and get in **good trouble**, necessary trouble."

—John Lewis

Thurgood Marshall
Thurgood Marshall was the head of the NAACP Legal Defense and Education Fund. In *Brown v. Board of Education*, he argued before the Supreme Court that "separate but equal" school systems were unconstitutional. In 1967, Thurgood Marshall became the first Black Supreme Court justice.

Some older leaders of the African American community in Nashville were not supportive of the students' protests. One of Lewis's heroes, the lawyer Thurgood Marshall, was among those who advised a different approach.

Marshall told the students that the way to create real change in America was through the court system. He did not believe the sit-ins would work.

Lewis was disappointed that Marshall did not understand the power of peaceful protest. The court system is slow to create change. It had taken decades for the Supreme Court to conclude that separating people based on race was wrong.

Lewis and his friends didn't have decades to wait for change. They wanted their communities to be truly free, now.

Lewis (left) speaking to a police officer during a Nashville demonstration, April 29, 1964

Protesters heading for City Hall in Nashville, led by Rev. C. T. Vivian, Diane Nash, and Bernard Lafayette, April 19, 1960

SNCC
SNCC (pronounced SNICK) was formed at the Raleigh Conference, a gathering of Black and white students from across the country who all wanted to end segregation in the US.

The students formed an organization called the Student Nonviolent Coordinating Committee (SNCC). The group planned a peaceful march. Thousands of protesters, white and Black, marched to Nashville's city hall. Under intense pressure, Mayor West declared before the protesters that segregation was wrong.

Diane Nash
Diane Nash spearheaded some of the most successful nonviolent campaigns, such as the Nashville Student Movement and the Freedom Rides. She was awarded the Presidential Medal of Freedom in 2022.

New talks between the city of Nashville and the committee of Black leaders resulted in an agreement that would end segregation at lunch counters. On May 10, 1960, Black and white people sat side by side at lunch counters in Nashville. But lunch counters were only the beginning.

23

Careful Selection
Lewis had to apply to be a Freedom Rider. The application required an essay and recommendation letters to show that he was fit for the mission.

Congress of Racial Equality
CORE was founded in Chicago in 1942 by activists including James Farmer Jr., Bayard Rustin, George Houser, Homer Jack, and Bernice Fisher. Its mission today is "to bring about equality for all people regardless of race, creed, sex, age, disability, sexual orientation, religion or ethnic background."

FREEDOM RIDERS

Lewis believed in what he called the "spirit of history." He felt called to stand up for what was right. His next important choice was joining the Freedom Riders.

The Congress of Racial Equality (CORE) planned a protest against segregation in the interstate bus system. The Supreme Court had banned segregation on transportation between states. But these rules were not followed by many whites in southern states. Freedom Rides would put these laws to the test.

Freedom Riders on May 26, 1961

Lewis was one of 13 brave people, Black and white, on the first protest ride. The group was led by James Farmer Jr., one of CORE's founders.

James Farmer Jr.

On May 4, 1961, the Freedom Riders departed Washington, DC, on two buses. At first, things went well. Black riders were served sodas and were able to use restrooms in bus stations throughout Virginia and into North Carolina.

Starting a Tradition
The night before the Freedom Riders left Washington, DC, they shared a meal together at a Chinese restaurant. In later years, whenever the original Freedom Riders gathered for a reunion, they would eat Chinese food to honor that "last supper."

25

KKK

The Ku Klux Klan is a domestic terrorist group dedicated to white supremacy in the US. The group was founded after the Civil War to terrorize and inflict violence on Black people in order to maintain white power and control.

The firebombed bus in Anniston, Alabama

As they moved farther into the Deep South, the riders experienced more hatred and bigotry. When one rider tried to get his shoes shined at a "whites-only" barbershop inside the bus station in Charlotte, North Carolina, he was arrested.

In Rock Hill, Sorth Carolina, Lewis tried to enter the "whites-only" waiting room at the bus station. A gang of white men verbally abused and beat him.

In Anniston, Alabama, the KKK was waiting for the Freedom Riders.

The first bus was firebombed. As riders rushed to escape the burning bus, an armed white mob beat them severely. The second bus made it to Birmingham, only to be met by another angry mob. The mob beat the riders, who got no protection from police.

Lewis was not with the Freedom Riders on either of the buses that day. He had flown to Philadelphia for a job interview. He felt guilty that he had not been there.

Bull Connor
Eugene "Bull" Connor was the commissioner of public safety in Birmingham for 22 years. He used police dogs and fire hoses to attack protesters, and he let the KKK move freely in the city.

Freedom riders at the Birmingham bus station, May 1961

> "It was clear to me that if we allowed the Freedom Ride to stop at that point... the message would have been sent that all you have to do to stop a nonviolent campaign is inflict massive violence."
>
> —Diane Nash

The US government tried to negotiate with the Alabama state government for safe passage of the riders. Alabama Governor John Patterson, who was opposed to the riders' mission, said this was impossible. Farmer, the leader of the CORE Freedom Riders, decided that because of new threats, the bus rides needed to stop. The Freedom Riders took a flight to New Orleans. They had reached their final destination, but not the way they'd planned.

Lewis, however, was not going to give up so easily. He reached out to his friends in Nashville. He brought a new wave of Freedom Riders to Alabama.

Patterson got a judge to issue an order to stop the Freedom Riders from moving. But the eyes of the nation and the federal government were on Birmingham. So, Patterson assigned a team of Alabama State Troopers to escort them to the state capital, Montgomery.

Governor John Patterson
John Patterson was elected governor of Alabama in 1958. He was supported by the KKK during his campaign and throughout his term.

Freedom Riders getting ready to ride from New Orleans to Jackson, Mississippi, May 30, 1961

"Some men held him while white women clawed his face with their nails... I had to turn my head back because I just couldn't watch it."

—Freedom Rider Catherine Burks-Brooks, describing the attack on Jim Zwerg

At Montgomery's city limits, the state police abandoned the bus. At the bus station, there were no police to stop the hundreds of angry white people who stormed the bus. They carried baseball bats, rope, iron pipes, chains, and bricks—anything to hurt the Freedom Riders.

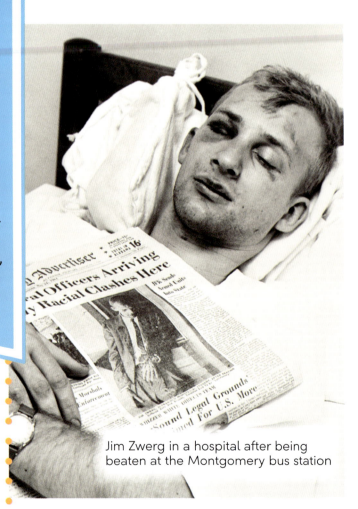

Jim Zwerg in a hospital after being beaten at the Montgomery bus station

Lewis and Zwerg after the attack

The violence overwhelmed the peaceful protesters. Rider Jim Zwerg was brutally beaten and knocked out. William Barbee suffered brain damage. Lewis was hit by a soda crate and knocked unconscious. Finally, the police arrived and broke up the angry mob.

The next day, US marshals were sent to control the situation. Many civil rights leaders across the country united behind the riders.

All Eyes on America
The violence against the Freedom Riders made national and international news. To many around the world, the US had been seen as a beacon of freedom. Allowing their people to be beaten like this put that reputation in doubt.

Mississippi Burning
In October 1962, James Meredith became the first Black student to enroll at the University of Mississippi. Thousands of white supremacists reacted violently to the action. US marshals, the US Army, and the Mississippi National Guard had to intervene to stop their attacks.

Not all civil rights leaders supported the Freedom Riders, particularly some in the older generation. But young leaders like Lewis and Nash had made this a youth movement. They were determined to get to the next, and possibly most dangerous, part of their journey: Mississippi. With a military escort, they left Montgomery on May 24.

People supporting the Freedom Riders in New York City, May 1961

 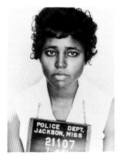  

At a bus station in Jackson, Mississippi, the Freedom Riders tried to use the bathrooms and waiting rooms reserved for white people. They were all arrested for trespassing. Lewis was imprisoned for more than a month.

But the Freedom Rides had taken on a life of their own. Hundreds of activists joined the effort, and the rides continued throughout 1961. Their actions forced the nation to look at what was happening to Black people in the Deep South.

Mug shots of jailed Freedom Riders, including Lewis (top left)

33

YOUNGEST OF THE BIG SIX

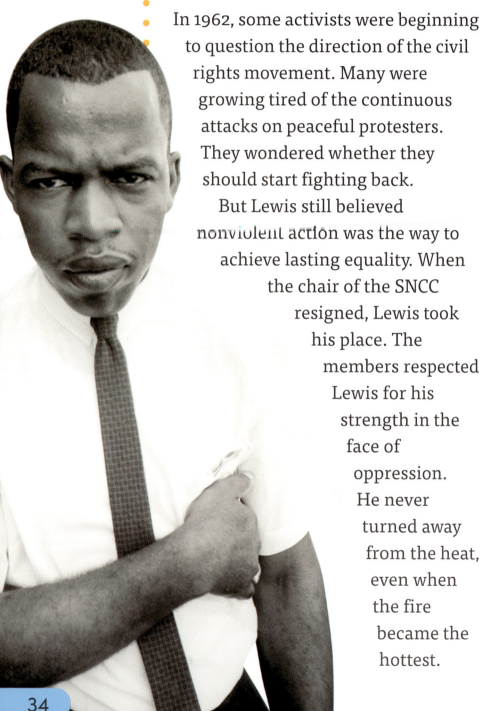

In 1962, some activists were beginning to question the direction of the civil rights movement. Many were growing tired of the continuous attacks on peaceful protesters. They wondered whether they should start fighting back. But Lewis still believed nonviolent action was the way to achieve lasting equality. When the chair of the SNCC resigned, Lewis took his place. The members respected Lewis for his strength in the face of oppression. He never turned away from the heat, even when the fire became the hottest.

The Big Six, March 6, 1963

Lewis began working with five other leaders, in a group that came to be known as the Big Six. Lewis was nervous about working with his heroes. He was by far the youngest of the group. But his fervent spirit and willingness to put himself in harm's way over and over had earned him a place among them.

The Big Six
John Lewis, Whitney Young, A. Philip Randolph, Martin Luther King Jr., James Farmer Jr., and Roy Wilkins would be remembered as the Big Six. All became renowned for their work to achieve equal rights for all Americans.

35

A March to Remember More than 250,000 people of all races took part in the March on Washington.

As chair of the SNCC, Lewis was invited to the White House in 1963. President John F. Kennedy wanted his support for a national civil rights bill that would desegregate public places nationwide. But the president also hoped to talk Lewis out of the big march he and other civil rights leaders were planning.

Lewis was shocked. He had expected the president's support for the march. But he was not afraid to move ahead without it.

Civil rights leaders meeting with President Kennedy and Vice President Johnson at the White House on August 28, 1963, the day of the March on Washington

Lincoln Memorial Speeches at the march were delivered from the steps of the Lincoln Memorial on August 28, 1963. This was 100 years after Lincoln's Emancipation Proclamation, which paved the way for the abolition of slavery in the US.

Lewis and the organizers of the march refused Kennedy's request. Planning for the March on Washington for Jobs and Freedom went ahead. The march would bring thousands of Americans who believed in equal rights together in Washington, DC.

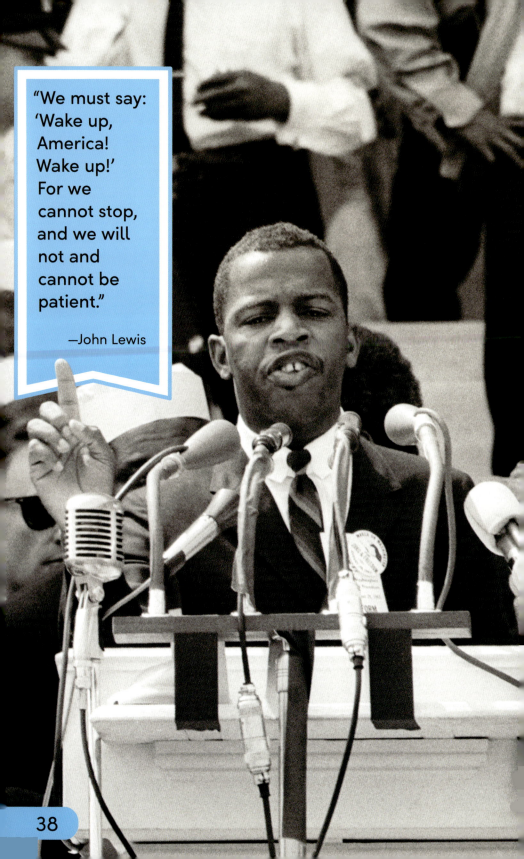

"We must say: 'Wake up, America! Wake up!' For we cannot stop, and we will not and cannot be patient."

—John Lewis

Lewis was the youngest speaker at the march. He talked about how many African Americans were unfairly paid, or without work, and starving. He noted ways their voting rights were being oppressed. And he described the necessity for them to be accepted in American society and to receive the same treatment as their white counterparts.

"We will march with the spirit of love and with the spirit of dignity that we have shown here today. By the force of our demands, our determination, and our numbers, we shall splinter the segregated South into a thousand pieces and put them together in the image of God and democracy. We must say: 'Wake up, America!'"

Lessons in Diplomacy
The first draft of Lewis's speech said that Kennedy's civil rights bill was "too little, too late." But other members of the Big Six encouraged him to soften his language. They wanted to work with the Kennedy administration to make changes for the whole country.

From Kennedy to Johnson
On November 22, 1963, President John F. Kennedy was assassinated. Vice President Lyndon B. Johnson took his place, then won the presidential election of 1964.

BLOODY SUNDAY AND BEYOND

Following the march, Lewis and the SNCC turned their focus back to the South. In Selma, Alabama, they were working to ensure the voting rights of African Americans. The city's local laws and practices made it difficult to register to vote. Only around 2 percent of eligible Black citizens were registered.

In February 1965, Jimmie Lee Jackson, a deacon at his church and a civil rights advocate, was taking

part in a protest march when Alabama State Troopers began beating protesters. As Jackson tried to protect his mother, a trooper shot him. Jackson died a week later.

Jackson's death ignited a fire under Lewis and other leaders, including Hosea Williams. They planned a march from Selma to Montgomery, where they hoped to speak with the governor. They had led protests in Alabama before, so they knew to expect resistance from government authorities. But the violence they met was worse than they could have imagined.

Two Minute Warning
Marchers face a line of state troopers in Selma on March 7, 1965. This picture, taken by Spider Martin, is called "Two Minute Warning," because the troopers had just told the marchers they had two minutes to turn around.

Civil Rights Act of 1964

In 1964, Johnson signed the Civil Rights Act that Kennedy had championed. This outlawed discrimination based on race, color, sex, religion, or nationality. This was a huge step, but it did little to eliminate extreme racist views in the Deep South.

As about 600 marchers crossed Selma's Edmund Pettus Bridge on Sunday, March 7, they encountered a wall of Alabama State Troopers with riot shields and clubs, some on horseback. They were determined to halt the marchers' advance.

Sheriff Jim Clark said the march was "unlawful." He commanded the peaceful protesters to turn around. Lewis and his allies stopped, but they did not turn back.

State troopers used tear gas to break up the march.

State troopers in gas masks attacking marchers in Selma. Lewis is on the right, wearing a backpack.

About one minute after they had given the marchers a two-minute warning, the state troopers attacked the marchers with brutal violence, determined to force Black people to understand that they were second-class citizens. Dozens of people were badly injured. Lewis's head was bashed in by a club. His skull was fractured, and he suffered a serious concussion.

Lewis in the hospital the day after the attack in Selma

Amelia Boynton Robinson (1911–2015)
One of the activists behind the march from Selma was Amelia Boynton Robinson. Robinson worked for the government to teach Black farmers to improve agriculture, led initiatives to educate Black Americans on voting rights, and was the first Black woman to run for Congress in Alabama, in 1964.

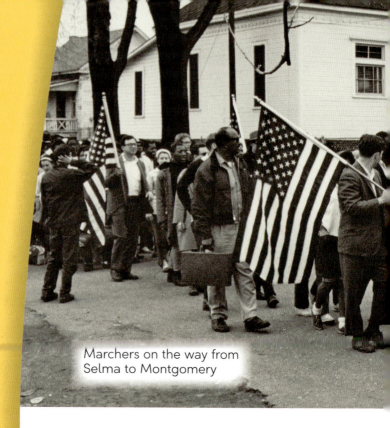

Marchers on the way from Selma to Montgomery

The violence in Selma shocked the nation. Johnson declared it unacceptable. He said, "It is the effort of American Negroes to secure for themselves the full blessings of American life. Their cause must be our cause, too. Because it is not just Negroes, but really it is all of us, who must overcome the crippling legacy of bigotry and injustice. And we shall overcome."

Less than a week later, Lewis testified before a federal judge, explaining what had happened in Selma. The judge said the people had the constitutional right to march. Finally, on March 21, 1965, thousands of activists joined Lewis, King, and other civil rights leaders on the five-day, 54-mile march from Selma to Montgomery. By the time they reached the state capital, the march had grown to 25,000 people who believed in equal voting rights for all.

Lewis speaking at the end of the march to Montgomery, March 25, 1965

Voting Rights Act of 1965

Johnson's Voting Rights Act made it easier for Black people to register to vote. They could no longer be charged a tax to vote or be forced to take a reading test before registering. By the end of the year, a quarter of a million new Black voters had been registered.

Five months after the Selma march, Johnson signed the Voting Rights Act of 1965 into law. At the same time, however, cracks were forming in the SNCC. New members were impatient with the nonviolent approach that had brought them so much success. This shift in ideals went against Lewis's core beliefs. In 1966, he resigned from the SNCC.

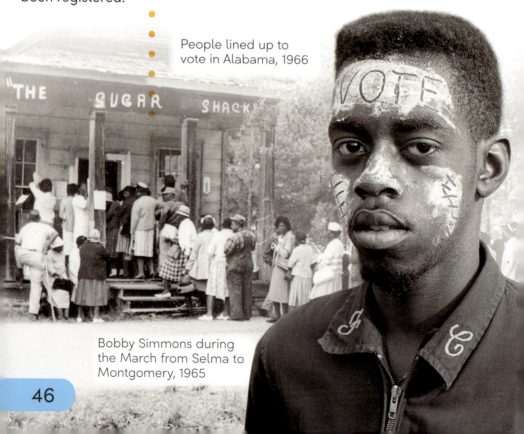

People lined up to vote in Alabama, 1966

Bobby Simmons during the March from Selma to Montgomery, 1965

46

Lewis during a "sit-down" protest in June 1965

Lewis was saddened to see the movement turning away from the foundations that had drawn him in. He was still committed to the idea of nonviolent protest.

During this time, he met the love of his life, Lillian Miles. John felt complete with Lillian in his life. In 1968, they were married. Eight years later, their family grew to include their son, John-Miles Lewis.

Lillian Miles Lewis
Lillian Miles was a volunteer with the Peace Corps and worked as a librarian before she met John in 1967. She was involved in local politics, and she would encourage John to run for office.

John and Lillian in 1986

Vietnam War
The Vietnam War brought much division to the United States, particularly in the Black community. While African Americans made up only about 12.5 percent of the US population, they accounted for 16.3 percent of the armed forces and up to 25 percent of enlisted men in the US Army during the Vietnam War. Yet only 2 percent of military officers were Black.

MOVING TOWARD GOVERNMENT

In 1968, Lewis took a job with Robert Kennedy's presidential campaign. Robert was the brother of John F. Kennedy. He opposed the war in Vietnam. He wanted to see Black and white communities unite.

On April 4, 1968, Lewis was working with Kennedy's campaign when King was assassinated. Lewis was devastated. He felt he lost a part of himself when King died. United in grief, Lewis and Kennedy became close friends.

"I think our country and the world community would have been much better if he had lived.... He would have been a force in bringing together the young people of the world."

—John Lewis, on the 50th anniversary of Robert Kennedy's death

It seemed likely that Kennedy would win the presidential election in November. But on June 5, the nation was shocked by another assassination: Robert Kennedy was shot. He died the next day.

Lewis was there with Kennedy the night he was shot. Lewis said he cried on the flight home, "all the way from Los Angeles to Atlanta." The back-to-back deaths of his dear friends shook John to his core.

The Lewises headed for a victory party in 1986

On the Home Front
Once Lewis was elected, he was often in Washington, DC. Lillian remained his closest adviser but stayed mostly in Atlanta, where she worked as an administrator at Clark Atlanta University, an HBCU.

Inspired by Robert Kennedy, Lewis spent the next several years working on voter registration, becoming the director of the Voter Education Project. Under President Jimmy Carter, he served as director of the federal agency that oversaw the Peace Corps.

Lewis had seen firsthand how politics could help empower people of all races. He felt called to run for office. Lillian encouraged him and helped him campaign.

Lewis first served on the Atlanta City Council. In 1986, he ran for the US House of Representatives and won. It was the first of 17 consecutive elections he would win for this position. He served in the House for 33 years—the rest of his life.

Lewis in front of City Hall in Atlanta, 1982

John the Unknown

When Lewis first ran for Congress, the *Atlanta Constitution* newspaper called him "John the Unknown." They said, "He seems to take more pride in, gain more satisfaction from, accomplishing deeds than in speaking of them.... But we prefer John the Unknown, who is known by millions as a hardworking, dedicated man, sensitive to human problems, capable of helping to solve these problems."

THE CONSCIENCE OF CONGRESS

During his distinguished political career, Lewis earned the nickname "the Conscience of Congress." He chose to stand on the side of what he believed was right.

Lewis felt that he carried the legacy of the civil rights movement. He saw serving his country this way as both a privilege and a great responsibility.

Lewis did not always have the votes in Congress to create the laws he wanted. But that didn't stop him from standing up for what he believed was right.

"What fruit will our actions bear, not just for us but for our children? And not just for the children of our own land, but the children of the West, and the Middle East, and the world? It is the children, our little boys and girls, who must live with the consequences of our war."

—John Lewis

Lewis testifying in Congress about the contributions of enslaved builders to the construction of the U.S. Capitol, November 2007

In 1994, Congress passed the Violent Crime Control and Law Enforcement Act. Lewis believed the law targeted people of color living in inner cities, and he spoke out and voted against it.

In 1991, Lewis voted against US involvement in the Gulf War. In 2002, he argued against the US invasion of Iraq. He believed war was wrong and that the US should seek peaceful solutions.

In 2008, Lewis supported Barack Obama's run for president. Without the dangerous and difficult work Lewis and his allies in the civil rights movement had done for decades, America might never have seen a Black person as president.

Despite Obama's presidency, Lewis knew there was much more work to be done in the fight for equality. Even today, a disproportionate percentage of the US prison population is Black. Black people continue to be killed

> "Generations from now, when parents teach their children what is meant by courage, the story of John Lewis will come to mind—an American who knew that change could not wait for some other person or some other time."
>
> —Barack Obama

Obama and Lewis in 2015, on the 50th anniversary of Bloody Sunday

The floor of the House of Representatives

by police at a much higher rate than white people. Voting is still more difficult for Black Americans in some places.

Lewis tried on multiple occasions to pass new laws about voting rights, but without success. Then, he led the charge to extend the 1965 Voting Rights Act, which continued some protections of voting rights. But a 2013 Supreme Court ruling allowed states to make laws that make it harder to vote. The fight continued.

US Congress
The US Congress makes laws for all Americans. It has two branches: the Senate and the House of Representatives. The House has 435 members, representing people of different districts within each state, while the Senate has 100 members, two from each state.

Medal of Freedom
In 2011, President Barack Obama gave Lewis the Presidential Medal of Freedom, the highest award a civilian can earn in the US.

Lewis shared his wisdom from years of nonviolent protests with a new generation of leaders in Congress. In 2013, he was arrested while leading a sit-in for immigration reform at the US Capitol. In 2016, when Congress failed to pass gun-control legislation after a mass shooting targeting the LGBTQ community, Lewis led a congressional sit-in.

Lewis wanted to keep history alive in the minds of younger Americans. In 1998, he worked with the Faith & Politics Institute to launch what became a yearly pilgrimage to Birmingham, Montgomery, and Selma. Congresspeople from all parties joined him to honor the courage of the brave Americans who'd worked to ensure civil rights.

Lewis also worked for years to help create the National Museum of African American History and Culture in Washington, DC. The museum has 10 floors of exhibits sharing the complex history and rich culture of Black life in the US.

Michelle Obama, John Lewis, Barack Obama, and Amelia Boynton Robinson leading a march on the 50th anniversary of Bloody Sunday, March 7, 2015

Award-Winning Author
With co-author Andrew Aydin, Lewis wrote *March*, an award-winning autobiographical graphic novel about his work in the civil rights movement. Two of the three volumes, illustrated by Nate Powell, rose to number #1 on the *New York Times* bestseller list.

Lewis with Representative Maxine Waters (right) during a voting rights rally in 2005

Throughout his life, Lewis continued to teach others to practice nonviolent resistance. He taught people to rely on empathy and love for all, even—or especially—those who do wrong.

"If you have someone attacking you, beating you, spitting on you, you have to think of that person," Lewis said. "Years ago, that person was an innocent child, an innocent little baby. What happened? Did something go wrong? Did someone teach that person to hate, to abuse others? So you try to appeal to the goodness of every human being, and you don't give up. You never give up on anyone."

"In my life I have done all I can to demonstrate that the way of peace, the way of love and nonviolence is the more excellent way. Now it is your turn to let freedom ring."

—John Lewis, 2020

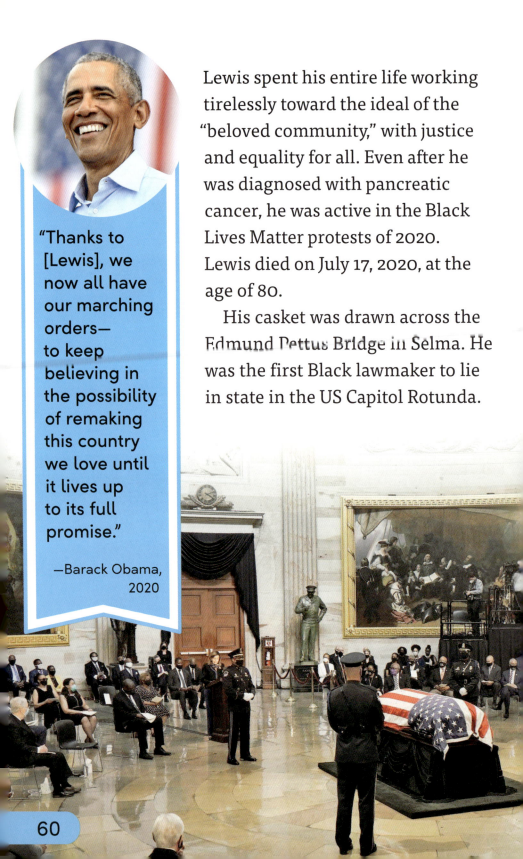

"Thanks to [Lewis], we now all have our marching orders—to keep believing in the possibility of remaking this country we love until it lives up to its full promise."

—Barack Obama, 2020

Lewis spent his entire life working tirelessly toward the ideal of the "beloved community," with justice and equality for all. Even after he was diagnosed with pancreatic cancer, he was active in the Black Lives Matter protests of 2020. Lewis died on July 17, 2020, at the age of 80.

His casket was drawn across the Edmund Pettus Bridge in Selma. He was the first Black lawmaker to lie in state in the US Capitol Rotunda.

Lewis believed that all people deserve to be treated with dignity. Because he did not see this happening in America, he chose to serve others by working to achieve it. This choice helped shape the lives of generations.

John Lewis and his "good trouble" surely accomplished a great deal of good in his remarkable life.

Honoring Lewis In 2024, the John Lewis Memorial by Jamaican sculptor Basil Watson replaced a Confederate monument in Decatur Square, outside Atlanta.

GLOSSARY

Activism
Work that's done to create social change or changes in laws and policies

Bigotry
Intolerance for opinions, beliefs, or identities that are different from one's own

Campaign
To engage in a series of actions designed to bring a particular result

Civil rights
Rights that promise equal opportunities and fair treatment for all people regardless of their race, sex, gender, religion, or nationality

Civil War
A war fought in America from 1861 to 1865, between Americans in northern states and Americans in southern states, primarily over the issue of slavery

Dignity
A sense of self-worth and self-respect

Discrimination
When people are treated unfairly because of their race, religion, or gender

Injustice
Unfair treatment

Jim Crow laws
Laws that enforced racial segregation and discrimination in the southern US after the Civil War

Legacy
What a person does or accomplishes during their life that affects future generations

Mob
A large and disorderly crowd that wants to cause trouble or harm

Movement
People working together for a cause

NAACP
The National Association for the Advancement of Colored People, an American organization created in 1909 to fight discrimination

Peace Corps
A US government program that sends volunteers to help in developing countries

Protest
To act or speak to change something considered to be wrong

Racist
Believing in or giving unfair treatment based on race or skin color

Register
To officially sign up to do something, such as voting

Segregation
Separation of people by their race or skin color

Sit-in
An occupation of a building by people protesting an injustice

INDEX

Aydin, Andrew 58
Barbee, William 31
Big Six 34–39
Birmingham, Alabama 27, 28, 29, 56
Blair, Ezell A., Jr. 14
Bloody Sunday 40–45, 54, 57
Brown v. Board of Education (1954) 12, 20
Burks-Brooks, Catherine 30
buses *see* Freedom Riders
Carter, Jimmy 50
Civil Rights Act 36, 39, 42
Clark, Jim 42
community 8–9, 60
Congress of Racial Equality (CORE) 24–33
Congress (US) 50–53, 55–56, 60
Connor, Eugene "Bull" 27
desegregation *see* segregation and desegregation
Farmer, James, Jr. 24, 25, 28, 35
Fisher, Bernice 24
Foote, Dennis 17
Freedom Riders 23, 24–33
Houser, George 24
Hunt, O. D. 17
Jack, Homer 24
Jackson, Jimmie Lee 40–41
Jackson, Mississippi 29, 33
"Jim Crow" laws 10
Johnson, Lyndon B. 37, 40, 42, 44, 46
Kennedy, John F. 36, 37, 39, 40, 42, 48
Kennedy, Robert 48–50
King, Martin Luther, Jr. 11–12, 16, 35, 45, 48
Ku Klux Klan (KKK) 26, 27, 29
Lafayette, Bernard 14, 22
Lawson, James 14, 16, 17
Lewis, John
    arrests 17, 18, 33, 56

childhood 8–12
college 12–13
death 60
Freedom Rides 23, 24–33
honors 56, 60, 61
Kennedy (Robert) campaign 48–49
March 58
March on Washington 37–39
marriage 47
Selma to Montgomery march 41–43, 45
sit-ins 5
SNCC leadership 34–36, 46
US Congress 50–53, 55–56
words of 15, 16, 19, 38, 49, 52, 59
Lewis, John-Miles 47
Lewis, Lillian Miles 47, 50
March (graphic novel) 58
March on Washington 36–39
Marshall, Thurgood 20
Martin, Spider 41
McCain, Franklin 14
McNeil, Joseph 14
Meredith, James 32
Montgomery, Alabama 12, 16, 29–32, 41–46, 56
NAACP 20
Nash, Diane 22, 23, 28, 32
Nashville, Tennessee 5, 13–23
nonviolent resistance 11, 14, 16, 34, 46, 47, 56, 58–59
Obama, Barack 54, 56, 57, 60
Obama, Michelle 57
Parks, Rosa 16
Patterson, John 28, 29
Peace Corps 50
Powell, Nate 58
Presidential Medal of Freedom 56
Randolph, A. Philip 35

Richmond, David 14
Robinson, Amelia Boynton 44, 57
Rustin, Bayard 24
segregation and desegregation
    barbershops 26
    buses and stations 24, 26, 33
    Civil Rights Act 36, 39, 42
    drinking fountains 10
    Freedom Rides 23, 24–33
    Nashville 15, 19
    restaurants 14, 15, 19, 23
    schools 12, 20
    University of Mississippi 32
Selma, Alabama 40–46, 56, 60
sharecroppers 8, 9
Simmons, Bobby 46
sit-ins 5, 14, 15, 56
Smith, Kelly Miller 14
SNCC 22, 34–36, 40, 46
Supreme Court (US) 12, 20, 24, 55
Till, Emmett 11
Troy University 12, 13
US House of Representatives 50–53, 55–56, 60
US Supreme Court 12, 20, 24, 55
Vietnam War 48
Vivian, C.T. 22
voting rights 39, 40, 44, 46, 50, 55, 58
Voting Rights Act 46, 55
Washington, DC 25, 36–39
Waters, Maxine 58
Watson, Basil 61
West, Ben 19, 22
white supremacists 26, 27, 29, 32
Wilkins, Roy 35
Williams, Hosea 41
Young, Whitney 35
Zwerg, Jim 30, 31

QUIZ

Answer the questions to see what you have learned. Check your answers in the key below.

1. Where did John Lewis first participate in lunch counter sit-ins?

2. What were the Black and white protesters who rode buses together into the Deep South called?

3. What did March 7, 1965, the day when peaceful marchers were beaten in Selma, come to be known as?

4. How many years did John Lewis serve in Congress?

5. What kind of trouble did John Lewis encourage people to get into?

1. Nashville 2. Freedom Riders 3. Bloody Sunday 4. 33
5. Good trouble